CURRENT
SCIENCE®

Alien
INVASION

Invasive Species Become Major Menaces

By Cari Jackson

Reading Consultant: Cecilia Minden-Cupp, Ph.D., Literacy Specialist
Science Curriculum Content Consultant: Debra Voege, M.A.

Gareth Stevens
Publishing

Please visit our web site at **www.garethstevens.com**.
For a free color catalog describing Gareth Stevens Publishing's list of
high-quality books, call 1-800-542-2595 (USA) or 1-800-387-3178 (Canada).
Gareth Stevens Publishing's fax: 1-877-542-2596

Library of Congress Cataloging-in-Publication Data

Jackson, Cari.
    Alien invasion : invasive species become major menaces / by Cari Jackson ;
    reading consultant, Cecilia Minden-Cupp ; science curriculum content consultant,
    Debra Voege.
        p. cm. — (Current science)
    Includes bibliographical references and index.
    ISBN-10: 1-4339-2057-3   ISBN-13: 978-1-4339-2057-8 (lib. bdg.)
    1. Biological invasions—Juvenile literature. 2. Invasive plants—Juvenile literature.
    3. Nonindigenous pests—Juvenile literature. I. Title.
    QH353.J33   2010
    577'.18—dc22   2009002279

This edition first published in 2010 by
Gareth Stevens Publishing
A Weekly Reader® Company
1 Reader's Digest Road
Pleasantville, NY 10570-7000 USA

Current Science™ is a trademark of Weekly Reader Corporation. Used under license.

Executive Managing Editor: Lisa M. Herrington
Senior Editor: Barbara Bakowski
Cover Designer: Keith Plechaty

Created by **Q2AMedia**
Editor: Jessica Cohn
Art Director: Rahul Dhiman
Designers: Harleen Mehta, Ranjan Singh Garsa
Photo Researcher: Kamal Kumar
Illustrators: Indranil Ganguly, Rohit Sharma

Photo credits (t = top; b = bottom; c = center; l = left; r = right):
Alexander Haas/imagequestmarine.com: cover, Rich Cary/Shutterstock: title page, Heidi & Hans-Juergen
Koch/Minden Pictures: 4, Nikita Zasypkyn/Dreamstime: 5, Tim Markley/Dreamstime: 6-7, Kletr/Shutterstock:
6c, U.S. Department of Agriculture: 6bl, Marevision/Photolibrary: 8, J-Photo Styles/Istockphoto: 9t, USGS/
Florida Integrated Science Center: 9b, Andrei Nekrassov/Shutterstock: 10tl, Dave Brenner/Michigan Sea
Grant: 10tr, Dreamstime: 10b, Michael Pettigrew/Shutterstock: 11t, Terry Alexander/Shutterstock: 11c, Sven
Weber/Fotolia: 11b, Ed Reschke/Photolibrary: 12, Deborah Benbrook/123RF: 13t, Global Photographers/
Bigstockphoto: 13b, Ian Holland/Shutterstock: 14t, John Carleton/Shutterstock: 14b, Shawn Low/Dreamstime:
15t, Michael & Patricia Fogden/Corbis: 15b, Christopher Howey/Dreamstime: 16, Galen Rowell/Corbis 17t,
Derek Rogers/Dreamstime: 17b, Jonathan Wood/Getty Images: 18, Formosan Fish/Shutterstock: 19t, Vladimir
Wrangel/Shutterstock: 19c, Thomas E. Hinds/USDA Forest Service: 20, Watershedcouncil: 21, Joe Giblin/
Associated Press: 22, Kenneth William Caleno/Shutterstock: 23, David Cappaert, Michigan State University:
24t, David Cappaert/Photolibrary: 24b, Er. Degginger/Photolibrary: 25t, Armando Frazao/Istockphoto: 25b,
Irochka T./Istockphoto: 26, Electric Head Inc./Istockphoto: 27t, Courtney Miller, Galveston Bay Foundation:
27b, James Gathany/CDC: 28, Tony Campbell/Shutterstock: 29, Goran Cakmazovic/Shutterstock: 30, Jen
Chase, Colorado State Forest Service/Associated Press: 32, Marhow/Bigstockphoto: 33t, Shutterstock: 33b,
Alistair Scott/Dreamstime: 34, James R. Tourtellotte/Canine Enforcement Training Center: 35, Shutterstock:
36cl, Scott Bauer, USDA Agricultural Research Service: 36b, U.S. Department of Agriculture: 37, Istockphoto:
37bl, Bill Waldman/Alamy: 38, NOAA Photo Library: 39t, John Good/nps.gov: 39b, Barry Winiker/Photolibrary:
40-41, Fotolia: 42, Lynn Stone/Photolibrary: 43, Heidi Keuler: 44, Irochka T./Istockphoto: 47
Q2AMedia Art Bank: 6t, 7, 21, 31, 33, 41, 45

Printed in the United States of America

1 2 3 4 5 6 7 8 9 12 11 10 09

CONTENTS

Words in **boldface** type are defined in the glossary.

Chapter 1

New Species on the Block

Aliens have landed on Earth, ready to destroy the planet. Does that sound like science fiction? A real-life alien invasion is taking place! The threat is not from outer space, though. We are being invaded by plants, animals, and other beings that already live here.

A BALANCED VIEW

Each creature and plant has a place in the natural order. Nature remains in balance when everything stays in its own **habitat**. When an **organism** moves into a different habitat, that organism can upset the balance.

KILLER FROGS INVADE

Thousands of African clawed frogs have taken over a park in San Francisco, California. Lily Pond in Golden Gate Park was once a peaceful place. Now the frogs are eating all the insects. When the frogs cannot find insects, they eat fish, turtles, and even other kinds of frogs. When they run out of those animals, they eat each other!

Scientists brought the frogs from Kenya to the United States to experiment on them. Then someone released the frogs into the park's pond. That was a bad idea!

The African clawed frogs are **invasive**. A plant or an animal that arrives in a new habitat is considered **exotic**, **non-native**, or **alien**. If the species causes harm, it is invasive.

In the frogs' **native** habitat, crocodiles and a limited food supply keep the number of frogs low. In Lily Pond, the clawed frogs have no natural enemies. The frogs have been able to damage the **ecosystem**, or community of organisms. Wildlife **biologists** are trying to destroy the frogs before the invaders escape the pond.

Invasive species can upset the natural balance in a habitat.

5

PESKY PLANTS

Alien animal species can be scary. Yet invasive plants are killers, too. They quickly affect **food webs**. Those webs connect the living things in ecosystems. The wrong kind of plant can cause big problems. Many plants spread quickly and take up available space and water. Kudzu, for example, is a plant from Asia. It can grow 1 foot (30.5 centimeters) a day! Kudzu has covered thousands of acres of forest in the U.S. Southeast. Native plants die out. Insects and animals lose their favorite foods and habitats.

Strange but True

Invasive insects can make plenty of trouble. In the 1970s, Christmas trees sent to the island of Hawaii carried insect hitchhikers. Yellow jackets hid in the branches. Yellow jackets eat insects. The yellow jackets put the native birds' food supply in danger. Fewer bugs **pollinated** fewer plants. The number of plants went down.

The Asian longhorn beetle destroys trees.

Ponds are in particular danger from invaders. Because most ponds are small, they can be taken over quickly.

INVISIBLE THREAT

Microbes are tiny organisms. The **fungus** that causes soybean rust is one example. The fungus, which came to the United States from Asia, attacks soybean plants. Whenever microbes arrive in a new habitat, disease experts get nervous. Scientists work quickly to contain the threat.

YOU DO IT!

Identify Invasive Plants in Your Yard

Be sure to have an adult help you with this activity.

What You Need

- photos of common invasive plants
- camera
- several small plastic bags
- scissors or plant clippers

What You Do

Step 1
Get a book or a magazine with photos of common invasive plants. Study the pictures.

Step 2
Go outdoors. With an adult, look for plants that match the photos. Make sure you are in a place where you can take plant cuttings.

Step 3
Take a picture, or cut off a small piece of the plant. This will help you identify it.

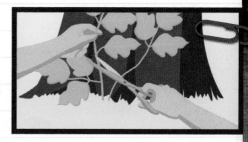

Step 4
Write the plant name and where you saw it.

What Happened?
If you found an invasive species, contact your local Fish and Wildlife Service. Find out more about invasive species in your area.

Round gobies have
an invasive appetite!

UNDERWATER LIFE

Government groups pay close attention to invasive species in U.S. waters. Our rivers have already been hurt by **pollution**. Almost 98 percent of our freshwater is polluted. Now most water species are rare or extinct. When alien species invade our waters, the ecosystem suffers even more.

NATURE'S BULLIES

One of the biggest offenders is only about 1 inch (2.5 cm) long. What is this mini-monster? It is the zebra mussel! Cargo ships from Europe carried the mussels with them.

Zebra mussels quickly took over. They crowded out native species of mussels. The zebra mussels clogged water pipes at electrical power plants. The mussels also caused die-offs of fish. The mussels broke up the **food chain**.

Round gobies arrived the same way. Round gobies are bottom-feeding fish. They eat zebra mussels, which is good. But they also eat food that native fish need. The round goby feeds on the eggs of lake trout, too. Fishermen lose money when there are fewer trout to catch.

AQUARIUM MANIA

People sometimes get **aquatic** plants from other countries. One example is the giant salvinia. It looks nice in aquariums or garden ponds, but it is a troublemaker. If just a tiny piece of giant salvinia gets into a large body of water, the plant grows out of control. It can cover the surface of lakes and streams. It can choke the water of oxygen. Fish and other organisms die.

Pet fish can also end up in rivers when owners release them. Sometimes fish are flushed down the toilet. They spill into nearby waters. In many parts of the country, irresponsible people have released the snakehead fish. This creepy-looking creature eats anything. It even eats birds and small mammals!

Strange but True

Alien species have found a new way to travel. They cruise on litter in the ocean. Marine animals have always hitched rides on natural **debris**, such as floating wood and coconut shells. Now, though, the amount of human-made trash in the ocean has grown. Creatures that usually spend their lives stuck to rocks or plants can now cross the ocean on floating plastic bottles. When the alien species arrive in a new land, they can become invasive.

Snakeheads threaten native fish, the fishing industry, and freshwater ecosystems.

Unwanted
Most Wanted
Invaders

Sea Lamprey
These killer fish came to the Great Lakes from the Atlantic Ocean. Their mouths are adapted to eating the insides of other fish!

Mouth

Cane Toad
These South American toads were brought to the United States in 1955 to eat bugs that were destroying sugarcane crops. They harm native species in Hawaii and Florida.

Pests are a problem nationwide. Here's a look at five invasive species that are putting native U.S. plants and animals at risk.

Asian Tiger Mosquito
These bugs hitched a ride to the southeastern United States in 1985 in tires shipped from Japan.

European Starling
People introduced these creatures into New York in 1890. The birds now fiercely compete with native species for nest locations throughout the country.

Nutria
These furry rodents look cute, but they damage crop areas along U.S. coastlines. Ranchers brought nutria from South America in the 1930s to raise them for their fur.

Chapter 2

Accidental Tourists

Gypsy moth

I nvasive plants and animals cause damage in their new homes. Humans are often to blame for the problem. Wherever humans explore, invasive species travel with them. As travel and trade increase, so do the opportunities for related problems.

Water hyacinth looks pretty…
until it takes over!

INVITED PESTS

In the 1860s, a scientist brought the gypsy moth to the United States. The scientist wanted to start a silk business. The gypsy moths produced no silk usable for cloth. Instead, the moths escaped. Baby moths traveled on lumber, which helped spread the moth to 18 states. These moths feed on 600 species of trees. Every year, they eat the leaves off a million acres of trees. The moths hurt fruit farms and the lumber industry.

LOOKS CAN KILL

Water hyacinth is a floating plant with a white flower. Gardeners use it to decorate ponds. When the plant finds its way into nearby waters, however, it spreads into a thick mat. **Algae** and underwater plants begin to die. The fish and animals that feed on them must find a new habitat, or they will die, too.

Fur Strikes Back

In the 1930s, furriers imported nutria for the fur trade. Some nutria escaped or were released. These animals cleared large areas of plants. Their activities cut the food supply for other animals. Nutria also destroyed valuable farm crops.

13

A ship like this one carried the Australian spotted jellyfish (right) to the U.S. Gulf.

STOWAWAYS

All kinds of invasive species travel on cargo ships. Many critters stow away in **ballast** water. The water is kept in tanks to help ships stay balanced. When a ship arrives at a port, it takes on water to balance the boat. At the next port, which may be thousands of miles away, the ship releases ballast water. Organisms in the water are dumped.

Ships around the world carry 10,000 species of creatures in their ballast water every day. The round goby and the zebra mussel came to the United States in ballast water. The sea lamprey entered the Great Lakes from the Atlantic Ocean through shipping canals.

HIDDEN HORRORS

Non-native insects and plant diseases like to hitch rides on imported plants. Hundreds of species of invasive insects and plant **pathogens** have set up new homes in North American forests. Sudden oak death and chestnut blight entered North America on garden plants. In fact, 18 of the 25 most damaging forest pests traveled on globe-trotting plants.

WORST-CASE SCENARIO

Some animals find creative ways to travel the world. The brown tree snake climbed up a plane's landing gear in Papua New Guinea. The snake landed in Guam, an island in the Pacific Ocean. With no natural **predators**, these poisonous snakes have eaten almost all of the animals in Guam's forests. They have eaten many people's pets. Some people have even been bitten in their sleep! The snakes also cause power outages when they climb onto telephone poles.

The brown tree snake has killed off nearly every native bird species in Guam.

This ant has a taste for wires.

Strange but True

Computer bugs are causing trouble in Australia. These bugs are not the kind that foul up software. These ants actually eat computers!

Singapore ants love electronics equipment. Scientists are not sure why. The ants may be attracted to the electrical currents. Perhaps the ants like the taste of the coating around the wires. These ants have crawled into newly purchased iPods and other electronics.

Australian tourists accidentally brought the ants home from Singapore. When the creatures landed in their new home, they set up large colonies. The hungry ants have even been known to eat through the rubber and wire in car engines!

15

THE WANDERERS

Over the past 30 years, airplane travel has increased. The human passengers do not travel alone. Tourists carry many microbes, plant seeds, and other invasive threats. A tourist who has walked in countryside where foot-and-mouth disease exists can carry the germs back home. If U.S. livestock become infected with that disease, farmers have to kill their entire herds.

A seed of Bermuda grass may stick to a shoe. A vacationer could accidentally carry the seed on his shoe to an island near Antarctica. Now the grass is a threat to the native plants on this far-off island. People plant Bermuda grass as ground cover because it spreads very quickly!

Tourists also secretly import fruits, plants, and animals. Those plants and animals may carry insect pests or diseases.

Non-native species have invaded the habitat of the Galápagos tortoise.

NO PLACE TO HIDE

Other than the ocean floor, there are few places on Earth where humans have not traveled. People have brought invasive species to many regions, including the Galápagos Islands. Those islands are off the coast of South America. People have introduced as many as 700 exotic species there. The new species include cats, pigs, and various invasive plants. Cats have killed birds and young animals. Pigs have destroyed the nests of tortoises and birds. Species on these islands cannot move to a new habitat. If an invader is more successful at claiming **natural resources**, the native species begin to die off.

Even frozen habitats are not safe from invaders.

Extreme Invaders

Even careful people can hurt ecosystems. Researchers are in Antarctica to study the **environment**. However, they also have accidentally released invasive species into the frozen land. You may think that species from other parts of Earth could never survive the freezing cold. **Extremophiles**, however, are organisms that do well in extreme environments. More extremophiles exist than you might think.

The researchers' dogs had canine distemper, a deadly microbe. The

dogs passed the microbe to seals. Many seals died. The deaths made the researchers think. Some planned studies require drilling through lake ice. Some scientists argue that drilling could introduce organisms into the lake below. No one knows how a new organism might affect that icy ecosystem.

17

PET THREATS

Many exotic pets pose a threat to native environments. Burmese pythons are imported from Southeast Asia. The snakes grow to almost 30 feet (9 meters) long. These killers can eat a full-grown deer. Yet some people think the snakes make good pets!

Irresponsible owners released their pythons into the Florida Everglades when their pythons grew too big. The snakes liked the weather in the Everglades. The snakes found each other, mated, and reproduced. These reptiles are the size of telephone poles. They dine on animals both large and small. The snakes eat **endangered species** and pets. They also pose a threat to drivers when they stretch across roads.

These killers could invade one-third of the United States. The snakes could spread throughout the warm southern states.

> **FAST FACT**
> More than 650 million illegal pets were brought to the United States in a recent three-year period.

Pet Burmese pythons took over parts of the Everglades after being released into the wild.

Lionfish are fun to watch in a fish tank. They are a menace to coral reefs, though.

Pet owners introduced snakehead fish to U.S. waters. A female snakehead lays 15,000 eggs at a time. She may lay eggs three times a year. The 1-inch-long (2.5-cm-long) babies (called fry) feed on fish eggs. Adult snakeheads easily beat out other fish for food.

These fish breathe air and can travel on land for up to three days. If a pet owner drops a snakehead into a pond, the fish can crawl on its front fins over land to a nearby river system. A river system can take the fish throughout many rivers, lakes, and streams.

FATAL FISH

Exotic fish are often a bad addition to an aquarium. Fish such as the lionfish eat every other fish in a tank. When fish owners realize they made a poor purchase, some of them release the creatures into the ocean. There, the lionfish eat native fish. Lionfish now live off the coast of the southeastern United States. The fish are ruining **coral reef** ecosystems. Yet all the U.S. lionfish may have come from just 10 fish that were bought as pets.

A WARM PLACE TO STAY

Invasive species are everywhere in the United States. However, warmer parts of the country provide better habitats for more species. For instance, the water hyacinth dies off during winters in the Northeast. Mild winters have allowed the plant to spread in the Southeast.

Invasive pests and disease threaten U.S. forests.

TRADING SPACES

Invasive species enter a country most often at places where trade takes place. A lot of Asian products enter the United States in the West. Western forests take a beating from invasive pests. Cargo ships also carry invasive species into the Great Lakes region. From there, invaders travel in rivers and streams throughout the central United States.

MAPPING AN INVASION

Zebra mussels started colonies in the Great Lakes. The invaders followed rivers and streams inland and spread throughout Michigan's waterways.

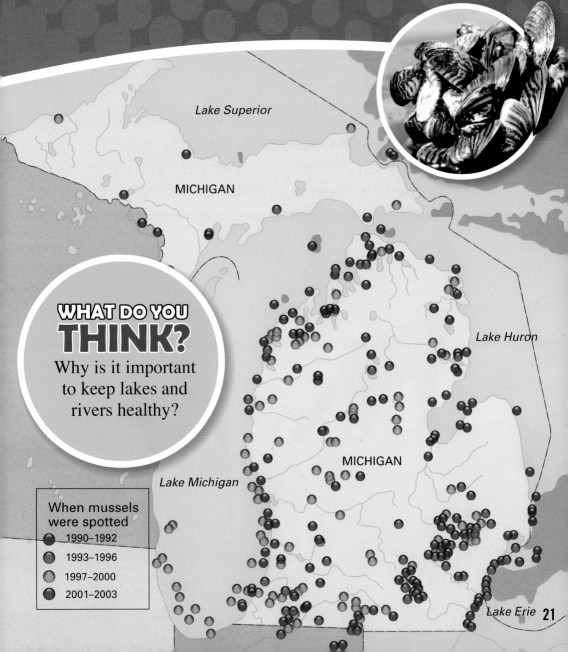

Lake Superior

MICHIGAN

WHAT DO YOU THINK?

Why is it important to keep lakes and rivers healthy?

Lake Huron

MICHIGAN

Lake Michigan

When mussels were spotted
- 1990–1992
- 1993–1996
- 1997–2000
- 2001–2003

Lake Erie **21**

Chapter 3

Bad Guests

Invasive species cause many problems in their new habitats. They compete for natural resources. They drive other species to their deaths. Sometimes, the invaders even hurt humans directly.

San Clemente
Island goats

DISTURBING THE PEACE

What happens when a new species enters a habitat? The native species must compete for the same space, water, food, and shelter. Invasive species can even kill off the natives. Consider the goats on San Clemente Island. The island is off the coast of California. The goats ate so much grass there that several grass species died.

One species can beat out another species for a food source. The ruffe, for example, is a fish that has invaded the Great Lakes. Ruffes feed on fish that native species need to eat. Native fish populations have started to die off.

THIRSTY WEED

Sometimes, one plant species drinks up most of the groundwater or takes over too much space. Yellow starthistle is a spiny plant that does both. It reproduces quickly and soaks up a lot of water. In a pasture, the plant replaces native grasses. Cows refuse to eat yellow starthistle. If a pasture is filled with the plant, farmers have to move their herds elsewhere. Yellow starthistle invasions cost the beef industry millions of dollars.

Strange but True

Majestic mute swans look like they belong in our country's ponds. They peacefully swim alongside ducks and geese. Yet the swans do not belong here. People brought the birds here to live in ponds and gardens. Unfortunately, the birds now harm many ecosystems.

Around the Chesapeake Bay, the swans eat tons of aquatic plants each year. The loss of those plants hurts native birds. Native birds move in and out of the area. They eat the plants for only a few months. The swans stay put, however. The swans feed on the plants year-round. When the native birds return, their food supply may be too low to support them.

VANISHING FISH FOOD?

Zebra mussels are hurting U.S. supplies of fish. About 700,000 of the invasive mussels can crowd into 1 square yard (0.8 square m). The mussels crowd out species of clams and other shellfish that people like to eat. The crowding costs the shellfish industry a great deal of money.

The zebra mussels also disturb the food chain. How? The mussels take in pollution from the water. Fish that eat the mussels are poisoned and die. The numbers of those fish, which are food for humans, have dropped.

THE FIGHT FOR OUR FORESTS

Millions of people rely on the lumber industry for their jobs. Wood-boring beetles are their enemies. The beetles destroy millions of acres of trees. The lumber industry suffers when so many trees die.

Emerald ash borer beetles traveled to the Midwest from Asia. They have eaten their way through 20 million ash trees in Michigan, Ohio, and Indiana. Eventually, emerald ash borer beetles could cost the United States billions of dollars.

Emerald ash borer **larvae** eat the inside of bark, hurting water flow in trees.

Boll weevils like to feed on cotton plants.

DOING DAMAGE

Invasive species cause harm in many different ways. Barnacles and mussels clog pipes that supply water to communities and industry. Honeybee mites are tiny creatures that can kill honeybees. A drop in the number of bees hurts crop production. Crops rely on bees for pollination. Many areas of the country depend on tourism from water recreation. But boaters and swimmers cannot enjoy waters that have been invaded by the water hyacinth or giant salvinia. Efforts to fight invasive species cost the United States billions of dollars every year.

FAST FACT
Coqui frogs from Puerto Rico have invaded Hawaii. Their extremely loud nighttime calls drive tourists away.

A Little Bug With a Big Appetite

The boll weevil is a funny-looking bug with a funny-sounding name. Yet no one laughed about its arrival. The boll weevil came to the United States in the early 1900s. This beetle feeds on all parts of the cotton plant. A female boll weevil lays 200 eggs every three weeks. Over 30 years, the pest spread through every cotton-producing state. The bug cost the cotton industry $15 billion. In the southern states, the boll weevil was a worse financial disaster than the Civil War!

Eventually, the government developed a plan to wipe out the pest. The program used **pesticides** combined with **pheromone** traps. Insects and animals produce chemicals called pheromones to attract a mate. The traps use a fake copy of the chemicals to lure and capture the bugs. The method has worked in many states. The boll weevil's days may be numbered.

25

STUNG BY NATURE

Some invasive species of plants and animals cause direct physical harm to people. Poison hemlock is an invasive plant with deadly seeds. Animals such as the Burmese python, which lives in Florida, can injure or kill people. Even some tiny insects can kill people and pets.

FRANKEN-BEES

In the 1950s, scientists in Brazil imported African honeybees, which are known for fighting. The scientists wanted to breed the fighters with the gentler European honeybee to create a better honey producer. Some of the African honeybees escaped.

Over the years, the offspring of those honeybees moved farther north. They reached the United States in 1990. The bees now live across the Southwest and in Florida.

The new kinds of honeybees are called killer bees. The new bees defend their nest against anything that comes within 50 feet (15 m). Sometimes the bees just make noise. At other times, though, they chase a target a long distance. They carry a poison no stronger than that of regular honeybees. Yet when killer bees attack, they do so in large numbers. Since the 1990s, more than 17 people in the United States have died from killer bee attacks.

Angry killer bees can stay on the attack for 24 hours.

A fire ant colony lives as one organism. Single ants cannot survive alone.

ANT ATTACKS!

In the 1930s, the red imported fire ant landed in Alabama, in a shipment from Brazil. The ants have since spread from North Carolina to California. These insects climb into air conditioners and stoplights and eat through the coating on wires. The ants damage crops. Their underground colonies cause roads and sidewalks to fall in. These nasty ants attack as a group. If a person or an animal steps on their mound, they grab on with their jaws. Again and again, they shoot poison into their victim's skin. Sometimes these attacks are deadly.

FAST FACT
The U.S. Department of Agriculture estimates that fire ants cost the country $5 billion a year.

Strange but True

The Brazilian pepper tree has deep green leaves and bright red berries. The tree looks like a great addition to any garden. Yet this tree comes from the same family as poison ivy. It causes **rashes** in many people who touch the leaves. People may break out if they touch the layer just below the bark, too. The Brazilian pepper tree also causes breathing problems in some people. The tree easily takes over new habitats. It has harmed a great deal of land in Florida.

INVASIVE GERMS

Tiny invaders hurt humans, too. A **virus** is a kind of microbe that can spread illness. In 1999, West Nile virus showed up around New York City. Dogs, birds, and humans became ill. Researchers think an **infected** bird or a mosquito carried the disease into the country. The mosquito is a common carrier. If it bites an infected bird and then bites a human, the person can catch the disease. Most people are strong enough to fight off the infection. A few people have died, however.

A DEADLY HUNTER

The Indian mongoose has hunted its way across Hawaii. Several species of animals have nearly disappeared because of this invader. The mongoose often carries the rabies virus. As the animal hunts, it spreads rabies to other animals. Rabies can spread from animals to humans through bites. Anyone exposed to the virus has to get several painful shots. If left untreated, rabies can kill people.

Mosquitoes can carry deadly microbes into the United States.

Wild birds carry the bird flu virus but do not get sick from it. The virus can kill poultry, such as chickens, ducks, and turkeys.

THREAT IN FLIGHT

A bird flu virus outbreak occurred in poultry in Asia in 2003. Wild birds caught the disease from poultry. Then the wild birds spread the virus as they traveled across the world. The disease rarely moves from birds to humans. Scientists worry, however, that the virus will change form. If so, the disease could sicken many people. Scientists are planning ways to protect the nation against this microbe.

WHAT DO YOU THINK?

How can scientists try to stop the spread of invasive viruses?

FAST FACT

About 50,000 non-native species live in the United States. Of those, 6,200 are invasive.

Chapter 4

A Global Problem

Invasive species are causing other species to die out. From 5 million to 30 million species exist on Earth. Yet scientists are alarmed by the number of species that are disappearing today.

BIODIVERSITY AT RISK

Biodiversity is the variety of species that live in an environment. Biodiversity is necessary for clean air and water and plentiful crops. Even the tiniest organisms provide services, such as breaking down wastes and improving soil.

When an invasive species moves into an area, the invader can take over. Other plants and animals lose their habitat. Scientists are worried about ladybugs for that reason.

Exotic species of ladybugs have come to the United States. The nine-spotted ladybug is now surrounded by new kinds of ladybugs. Will the new ones hurt the native ladybugs? Scientists are watching closely, because ladybugs control many kinds of pests that eat plants.

YOU DO IT!

Be a Biologist

What You Need
- jar with tiny holes in the lid
- camera
- paper and pencil
- computer

What You Do
Step 1
Go outside and look for ladybugs.

Step 2
Catch a ladybug in your jar. Put it in a freezer for a few minutes (no more than five minutes!) to slow its activity. With a digital camera, take a picture of the ladybug. Download the photos onto a computer. Record the time, date, location, and habitat where you saw the ladybug.

Step 3
Go online to **hosts.cce. cornell.edu/ladybeetles**. Upload your photos. Use the form provided at the web site. Type in the information you collected.

Step 4
Release your ladybug back into the wild.

What Happened?
You helped track the ladybug population! If you did not see any ladybugs, Cornell University researchers want to know that, too.

Western U.S. forests are under attack from alien beetles.

A WARMING WORLD

Global warming is an increase in the average temperature of Earth's surface over time. One of the biggest causes is the burning of **fossil fuels**, such as coal and gasoline. When fossil fuels burn, they let off gases that trap heat near Earth. If the temperature of Earth continues to increase, some species will lose their habitats. Experts say that invasive species are likely to move in.

A GROWING PROBLEM

The mountain pine beetle is native to western North America. The beetles kill millions of trees. People in the western United States struggle to control these pests. In Canada and Alaska, the beetles were not a problem in the past. The cold winters killed off any beetle babies. However, winters in Canada and Alaska are not as cold as they used to be. The mountain pine beetle can now survive in these northern areas.

GOOD OR BAD DECISION?

Many biologists worry that rising temperatures will cause certain species to die out. Some of these scientists want to move certain species to cooler places. The quino checkerspot butterfly is one such species. Other scientists say moving species is too risky. One species may be saved, but several others could be pushed out.

Burmese pythons can eat animals as large as pigs and deer.

Reptile on the Roam

As temperatures rise, Burmese pythons are spreading in the United States. Today, the Burmese python can survive only in the southern states. As Earth continues to warm, though, the snake could move northward.

UNITED STATES

- Burmese python cannot survive.
- Burmese python may be able to survive.
- Burmese python can survive.

33

Chapter 5

Fighting Back

Invasive species continue to spread throughout the United States and the world. In an effort to stop the spread, scientists are coming up with creative ways to fight back invaders.

Trained dogs sniff out invasive species.

PROVIDING PROTECTION

The United States Geological Survey (USGS) is a government organization. It researches environmental issues, including invasive species. The USGS provides tools that other groups can use to fight invasive species. The U.S. Fish and Wildlife Service (FWS) tracks invasive species nationwide. The FWS also runs programs to teach people about the problem. Other groups that work to protect the environment include the Environmental Protection Agency and the U.S. Department of Agriculture. Every state has a Department of Natural Resources (DNR). The DNR works with federal, or nationwide, agencies. It takes a wide group effort to combat invasive species.

Sniffing Out Trouble

U.S. Customs and Border Protection (CBP) is the group that inspects cargo and baggage coming across the nation's borders. Every year, the CBP catches tens of thousands of invasive species.

The CBP has about 1,200 trained specialists that work for treats. They are detector dogs that sniff out fruits, meats, and other items that may carry pests or diseases into the United States. Most detector dogs and their human handlers work at airports and seaports.

FRIENDLY ENEMIES

Species become invasive when they lack natural enemies in their new habitat. How do experts battle an invasive species? They often bring in an enemy! This method is called **biological control** (biocontrol, for short). For instance, certain grasshoppers feed on the water hyacinth. Scientists bring in grasshoppers to stop the spread of the invasive water plant. The scientists have to be careful that the "secret weapon" does not eat native plants as well!

GET YOUR GOAT

In Washington state, a plant called the thorny Himalayan blackberry plant took over a forest. Forest workers struggled to remove the thorny plant. Finally, they turned to goats for help. Goats have tough mouths that can chew through thorny plants. Goats also break down any seeds they eat, so plant seeds cannot spread through goats' waste. The goats worked quickly. Thirty goats had the area cleared in just a few weeks.

Himalayan blackberry plant

Goats provide chemical-free weed control!

WEEVIL WARRIOR

Melaleuca trees were introduced into southern Florida in 1906. People planted the thirsty trees to dry out the swampy Everglades. Since then, the trees have taken over thousands of acres of **wetlands**. The melaleuca is a threat to native plants and animals.

Now scientists want to rid the Everglades of the troublesome tree. So they went to the tree's home: Australia. There, the scientists found that a bug called the melaleuca weevil eats this tree. The scientists studied the bug for 10 years. In 2007, they sent the weevil into Florida forests. Scientists hope that the weevil and other bugs will get rid of the melaleuca trees.

Can a beetle from Down Under help save Florida's forests?

A Problem Becomes a Solution

Some of the waters around Washington state have invasive snails. The alien species is crowding out native clams and oysters. In 2005, officials in Olympia, Washington, did something to stop the problem.

Olympia receives a lot of rain. Runoff from streets and sidewalks floods streams when rain falls. People found out that snail shells could solve that problem. The people put the scoop-shaped shells underneath sidewalks. Instead of running straight into the sewer, the rain gets caught in the shells. The rainwater runs to the streams more slowly.

Oyster and clam diggers often collect the snails by accident. Now the diggers can sell the pests for money. Meanwhile, they make room in the ocean for native clams. Problem solved!

A mongoose will even attack poisonous snakes, such as cobras.

TWO WRONGS

Sometimes, experiments go wrong when biologists use a new species to get rid of an invasive species. In 1872, the island of Jamaica had a rat problem. Rats arrived on ships from Europe. The rats started ruining sugarcane crops. One man, W.B. Espeut, thought it made sense to bring in Indian mongooses, which eat rats. He encouraged people on other islands to do the same. Soon, mongooses were brought to the Hawaiian Islands, too. The experiment was a disaster, however.

The mongooses did little to get rid of the rats. Instead, they ate many other small animals. The mongooses caused several kinds of birds to die out. Meanwhile, the mongooses have no predators. Now many islands have problems with both pests— rats and mongooses!

WEEDS GONE WILD

Spotted knapweed is an invasive plant that grows in the western United States and Canada. It spreads quickly because it has no natural enemies. Scientists tried to wipe out the weed by introducing a kind of fly that eats the plant. Deer mice, however, gobbled up the baby flies in the knapweed flowers. The deer mice ate so many flies that the knapweed kept growing. Now the number of deer mice has increased. These furry creatures can carry a virus that can kill humans.

Efforts to control an invasive plant accidentally benefited deer mice in the western United States. The mice can carry disease.

Strange but True

The Mediterranean Sea has been invaded by algae! Algae are tiny organisms that live in water. In the 1980s, a special type of algae was used in aquarium tanks. Somehow the algae "escaped" into the Mediterranean. Now the organisms cover a large part of the seafloor. Fish do not eat the algae, which are poisonous to many sea animals.

Scientists are looking for a natural predator to control the algae. One possibility is a **sea slug** that eats the algae. Can the sea slug solve the problem? Or will it become a new pest? Scientists are racing to find the answer.

INVISIBLE FENCE

The Great Lakes are facing a big problem. Invasive species are in nearby rivers and lakes. How did the aliens get there? Fish farmers brought in Asian carp to control algae. Then floodwaters carried these fish into rivers. The carp are better than native fish at finding food. What if the invaders swim up a river and into the Great Lakes?

Fishing in the region brings in $5 billion a year. If the carp enter the lakes, there may be fewer fish for people to catch and eat.

To fight the carp, officials have built an underwater electrical field where Lake Michigan meets the Mississippi River. The fish receive a shock if they approach this wall.

Protecting our natural resources is important work.

40

WALL OF BUBBLES

Officials can also use sound to control invasive fish. Certain sounds bother fish. Engineers can build a "wall of sound" that stops unwanted fish from entering a waterway. Bubbles make the sound even louder for the fish. This setup needs little power to run. If there is a power failure, the sound-bubble wall can run on a backup machine.

SILVER BULLET

Scientists at the USGS are working on ideas that seem impossible. They are trying to come up with a type of fish poison that targets round gobies. Certain chemicals may trick only the round goby into eating the food. The scientists are still testing the idea. They want to make sure the fish poison does not affect native fish.

Deck

Hull

Ballast tank

Strange but True

Scientists have to find ways to control pests. Sometimes people find a solution by mistake. Shipbuilders had a problem with ballast water. The water sits in the tank of the ship for a long time. Slowly, the iron sides begin to rust. Oxygen is needed for rust to start. Shipbuilders decided to pump another gas into the tanks to remove the oxygen. The rust stopped building, but the shipbuilders saw another effect. Lack of oxygen killed 80 percent of all living things in the water in the tank. Invasive species such as the zebra mussel started losing their free ride.

Keep exotic fish in tanks, where they belong.

KNOWLEDGE IS POWER

One of the best weapons against the invaders is shared information. Sometimes, boaters unknowingly carry invasive species on their boats. People sometimes go fishing and accidentally use alien species as bait. The species can become invasive when introduced into the water. People can learn about responsible boating and fishing from the U.S. Fish and Wildlife Service.

BE RESPONSIBLE

People who keep aquarium fish or exotic pets need to be aware of how their hobbies can be harmful. If you tire of a difficult pet, never dump it into the wild. Pet owners can trade exotic fish with other people. You can talk to a veterinarian about the right steps to take.

RIGHT WAY TO CAMP

Many forests are filled with invasive plants. If you hike through a forest, clean your shoes before you move on. A seed could travel on your shoe. Always use firewood from close to your campsite. Do not transport wood to new areas. Invasive pests could travel in the wood and take over a forest.

PLANT A GARDEN OF DELIGHTS

Sure, purple loosestrife has beautiful purple flowers. But there is nothing pretty about the way it destroys threatened wetlands. Gardeners should choose native plants to decorate yards and public spaces. Find out what plants are native to your area.

DON'T BE A PEST!

Humans may be the worst invasive species of all. We travel into new areas. We use up natural resources. We carry pests to new lands. We crowd out native species. To act responsibly, we need to help keep places healthy. Then all species can find the food, shelter, and water they need to survive.

Protect the future by planting native species.

How You Can Help

Here are ways that you can help. Can you think of more?

- Fish with the right kind of bait.
- When camping, use firewood from nearby.
- Leave exotic animals in their natural habitats.
- When traveling, do not carry plants or fruit from country to country.
- Take part in projects that encourage the growth of native plants.

SCIENCE AT WORK

WILDLIFE BIOLOGIST

Job Description: Wildlife biologists study animals and wildlife. They specialize in wildlife research and management. They collect and study data to determine the effects of present and possible use of land and water areas.

Job Outlook: Competition for jobs is expected.
Earnings: $34,500 to $89,690, with a median income of $55,100

Source: Bureau of Labor Statistics

Conversation With a Wildlife Biologist

Heidi Keuler works for the U.S. Fish and Wildlife Service (FWS), a branch of the U.S. Department of the Interior. She specializes in fish.

HOW DID YOU BECOME A WILDLIFE BIOLOGIST?

In college, I got involved in the Wildlife Society [and attended a university program that taught about] loon and wolf tracking [and] soils and forestry. [Later,] I got a master's degree in aquatic science.

WHAT IS FIELDWORK LIKE?

We get in a little bit earlier and get our boats ready. We go over all of our equipment and make sure it's working. Then we go shocking [tapping fish with an electric pole to shock them to a stop]. They float to the top, [and we] weigh and measure them. Sometimes we do surgeries [on fish to place] an internal transmitter inside. Some fish are

migratory, so we want to track their movement. Then we release them back into the water.

WHAT IS YOUR FAVORITE PART OF THE JOB?

We helped restore lake sturgeon to [a reservation on the eastern side of Wisconsin]. It's amazing to have your hands on these fish that have been around since the times of the dinosaurs.

WHAT ADVICE CAN YOU GIVE INTERESTED KIDS?

Get outside and get involved with environmental groups. Join a scouting organization. If you volunteer, you can shadow professionals. The FWS even has a mentoring program.

FIND OUT MORE

BOOKS

Collard, Sneed B. III. *Science Warriors*: *The Battle Against Invasive Species* (Scientists in the Field). New York: Houghton Mifflin, 2008.

May, Suellen. *Invasive Aquatic and Wetland Plants* (Invasive Species). New York: Chelsea House, 2007.

Metz, Lorija. *What Can We Do About Invasive Species?* (Protecting Our Planet). New York: Rosen Publishing, 2009.

WEB SITES

Fish and Wildlife Service
www.fws.gov/invasives
Learn more about invasive species across the United States at the Fish and Wildlife Service's web site.

Sea Grant Nonindigenous Species
www.sgnis.org/kids
Be a super-sleuth and "Nab the Aquatic Invader" at this fun web site for kids.

Union of Concerned Scientists
www.ucsusa.org/invasive_species
The Union of Concerned Scientists shows what you can do to prevent invasive species from spreading throughout the world.

GLOSSARY

algae: simple water organisms with no roots or leaves

alien: a member of a species that is not native to its habitat

aquatic: relating to water

ballast: water carried in a tank on a ship to increase stability

biodiversity: the variety of life-forms in an ecosystem; short for *biological diversity*

biological control (biocontrol): the management of pests through life science

biologists: scientists who study living things

coral reef: underwater areas made of coral skeletons

debris: bits of rock, wood, and similar rubbish

ecosystem: all the living and nonliving things in an area

endangered species: species whose numbers are so small that the species is at risk of dying out

environment: the total surrounding conditions; the position of a species in its ecosystem

exotic: relating to a species that is not native to its habitat

extremophiles: organisms that thrive in extreme environments

food chain: the order in which organisms in a community eat one another

food webs: communities of organisms with several food chains

fossil fuels: fuels formed from plants and animals that died long ago

fungus: an organism such as a mold or yeast, which lives on another organism

global warming: the increase in the average temperature of Earth's atmosphere

habitat: the type of environment in which an organism lives

infected: invaded by a disease-causing agent

invasive: causing environmental or economic harm or injury

larvae: young forms of animals that change structure over time

microbes: microscopic living things

migratory: moving from one place to another

native: existing naturally in a particular ecosystem

natural resources: goods and services supplied by nature, such as food, water, and trees

non-native: relating to a species that is not native to its habitat

organism: any living thing

pathogens: things that cause disease, such as viruses

pesticides: chemicals used to kill pests

pheromone: a chemical released by some animals that affects the behavior of other animals

pollinated: fertilized a plant by putting pollen on it

pollution: harmful materials such as chemicals and wastes that dirty the air, water, or soil

predators: animals that hunt other animals for food

rashes: skin irritations

sea slug: a kind of water creature with gills and without a shell

virus: a kind of microbe that often causes disease

wetlands: land areas that are wet, such as marshes and swamps

INDEX

About the Author

Cari Jackson writes for children and adults. Her assignments have sent her around the world, to surf school, to circus school, and on a mission to test fireworks. She has interviewed artists, race car drivers, an Oscar winner, and a puppeteer. She lives in Brooklyn, New York, with her husband, her son, two dogs, and a cat.